AF529429

Evincepub
Publishing

Evincepub Publishing
Nehru Nagar, Bilaspur, Chhattisgarh 495001
First Published by Evincepub Publishing 2021

ISBN: 978-93-5446-296-2

Armories And Arsenals

Devarya Singhania

To you, and the warrior within.

Foreword

Could you have reconciled with your own chaos, knowing that the world around you lives in glee? Could you have embraced a path that promises nothing, knowing that the ones around you are rained upon with the sweetest of fruits? Would your journey have continued even when all around you reside on the island of success?

Amusing questions, aren't they?

For certain answers seem obvious on intuition, but it all sums up how well your deliberation commands your progress. For, not all are capable enough to reconcile with the key to their doom. It seeks a worthy contestant.

In a world where one witnesses such ambiguity, such uncertainity, do their problems hold the key to success? It is indeed exceedingly tumultuous to unleash your competency on those who continue to dominate.

When you're bundled with chaos, choked with accusations, and suffocated with illegitimacy, how would you wreak havoc? Would you break before the blinding reflection? Would you deafen the applause? Would you mute the roar?

What seems to the naked human eye as a preposterous riddle may well just be a requisite reconciliation. It's all about how you perceive this battle. You must reconcile with Chaos, for Chaos is waiting to asphyxiate you.

Does your prowess allow you to participate in such a limitless exchange?

You must not forget, worthy opponents stand before you - all with the same motive. Some may hold a stronger suit, some better wisdom.

Would you become intimidated? Would you still remain steady?

Does your armoury hold the necessary arsenal?

For when the battle commences, only Zeus shall walk out proud.
Shed a tear today, for tomorrow you must bleed.

Contents

Thursday Morning

A perfect abuse has not seen a better demonstration.
Maybe I am the culprit; maybe I am the victim.
Who knows? Who acknowledges?
An unleash of those who constantly parade on my soil.
Traitors. An unmatched love for havoc, an unending agitation of murder.

The clock strikes thirteen?
Maybe. But what good are those mediocre,
stranded spears for no one is there to be penetrated.
One slide, and the world panics. A mockery of sorts.
Tempting that ludicrous couple, inviting murder.

The Beauty and the Beast

Constantly bejeweled– as the mistress to the abuser of the misfortune,
She struggles, suffocates, surrounded by strangling venom,
Her voice distances, seeks refuge, constantly eroded, she rusts.

As her man, a very shrewd one indeed, takes a stance.
With his palm dripping with bucketed liquidity,
Losing grasp of his sanity.

His assertive arsenal takes shape, unleashes the devil within,
Exerts the miserable might, as she endures, disgruntled with disgust.
Envisioning her dignity set sail, as the scrutiny of her saree now stands laying at her daughter's feet.

She gasps! Breathless, yet the weaved assertion of patriarchy, censorship, gift her with the seemingly conclusive breaths.
His desires, his ambitions, his assertion,
Her sacrifice.

Oh, what a sacrifice it must be!
For he has now birthed a portrait of a thousand curses.
For they will loom ludicrously over his incompetence.

She seeks refuge. Assylum.
What a fitting name, she thinks.

His maniacal laugh daunts, haunts and taunts!
Her daughter, now the Ismene to the Oedipus.

Oh, for even Oedipus was not the cruelest.
The red ink flows, endlessly, shamelessly.

Nails, hammers, bricks - menial constructs, now cellular infusions.

Et tu, Brute?
She chuckles.

A heartfelt condolence to a literate.

stranded on the island, petalled by tumult.
encompassed by illiteracy,
desperation for labour.

his heart pounds,
shrieks, rumbles, and roars.
a dry throat, an ocean of paranoia.

as fish play the mockery of the poor,
he reconciles, foolishly lured,
he sets sail, sinks.

Custodial Juvenile

he does not like it here, he mumbles.
but he must persist, he cries.
all is but an ocean too deep, he thinks.
engulfed with delusion, he refuses.

those menacingly lurking waves eye his opacity,
he stood casually, now the haunt embraces.
a splatter of custody, a crash of inevitability.
an enveloping of guilt, the pride of victory.

Farmer, Soldier or Citizen, War Calls.

This agitatedly unending sense of disgust somehow pierces its way through,
The wail of a siren, the screams of the layman, the cry of the dog.
All seem so faint.
A bar, a restriction of sorts? It deafens my defense, simply magnificent.
Ah! That piercing, sharper than usual.
Bundled with an enormous arsenal of supposed instruments of literacy.
A cursed imprint on the glory of her beauty, a sign of demolition.

Unprecedented Halts to an Oppressive Democracy

As one is imprisoned and abandoned of their own freedom,
Paid for by their dignity,
Endured by their sacrifices,
Disrupted by their hope.

Curator of the masses, bless us with the blessings,
Mockery. For that is delusion; ours is rationality.
Incited by hope, a constant reiteration of it's viciousness.
Nevertheless, search for answers, for they stand anagrammed.

Perplexing, yes. But only since the additional chaos is present.
Ignore, and succeed.
Overthrow to overcome; they are deaf, blind, and mute.
Do not delude or be deluded.
Hope is a curse.

Hurled Abuse

A lushful land of that venomous deception.
In abundance, no less.
His control! Hurling abuses, yet *he* is the heir?
A rustic poison, now a remedy.
A deafening curse, now a prayer.
As it's shot above, tormenting the enchanting, beautiful
blankets of the cerulean sea.
Hurled abuse.

His demands exceed every challenge. For what?
Another venomous deception.
He reloads his gut-wrenchingly malignant decibel,
exercises the unfailing command.
That scar now bleeds excessively.
My constant appal at this perusal.
For why is my assignment so malicious? Hurled abuse.

You gamble on my prowess, you gamble on my sanity,
you assault me for your failure.
My master has tamed me into a figure which houses your
probable blessing.
A figure who is constantly imprisoned in a cubicle so
diminutive,
it mirrors my dignity.

Now, as I return to be assaulted again, you are gifted with a monetary exemplification.

Hurled abuse!

An Uncanny Shriek

despair fills his uncanny, shabby sorrow,
for his curiosity is always unfailing.

from a brawl to the adventure,
his resilience has endured all abuse.

no reward, abuse.
but he doesn't fear this mediocre punishment just yet,

for he knows not whether he *should* fear.
for the battle's definitely lost, and he knows not whether it'll be won,

as the siren wails again,
calling for a departure, the throne waits again.

his wais, his cries, now shunned into an opaque, soundless cave.
where the echoes fail to recover, and his feet fail to hold firm.

shall he attempt to embark and seek the faint glow?
or shall he let his miseries encompass his hope?

A Constant Chatter, the Inevitable Result

A fragile muttering, diminutive.
A faint chirp, a ghastly breath.

It fades away as my grasp tries to extend.
Zukunft, *Dunkel*, *Sterben*, all's gibberish.

Another assault greets this curse,
Zelfmoord, *Aanval*, *Misbruik*, gibberish again.

An irritation, persistent.
termites have grouped up, I suppose.

I fail to recognise, to register,
As those supposedly unfailing chants dominate my luxuries.

What curse it is to have such a privilege which
Prevents one's association with any intellect.

The Layman's Limerick

An endorsement of abuses,
The filth of their greed.
The reality of our dissonance,
The delusion to their intercede.

As rallies engulf our ever-so-fragile figures,
Abuses hurl and desolation flickers,
For all resources now seem exhausted,
Amateur, poor. The nation's hopes now frosted.

A poor recollection,
A fatal being,
Bound to be hated,
Like a limerick by a poet, inscribed and advocated.

Power

Amusing how particles invisible to the naked human eye can devastate a sphere believed to be the home of the superior within a blink of an eye.

Air, a concept we believe has given us the permission to progress is itself dominated by the toxicity given birth to by us, the apparent superior, by the toxicity

which stands firm as bars from a prison, dictating and guarding our freedom, for which without which we would and would not be able to dwell in continuity.

Something so invisible that we, using the arrogance of being superior, have jotted them down with mere ink made of the identical particles used to

poison and give birth, confirmed by ourselves that we are accurate and not even the collapse of a mountain or a tsunami of the sea could prevent us from being so?

It is due to this arrogance of ours that we will slash our throats and push ourselves into a pit, and it is due to this arrogance of ours that

We will create a path forward. Two options, yet none will be within our grasp. We have led ourselves into Nowhere and will refuse from not doing so.

We have declared ourselves to be superior, and yet thrive on being inferior. Judgements are feared, for they may be accurate. For they are accurate.

We are deluded into thinking that we can encapsulate our intellectual prowess, for we have none.

Look around, witness the destruction, reflect.

An Apology

I know my generation is not the most competent, erudite, edifice yet yours is no gem either! Now it's hard for me not to generalise, so I shall progress with what I can, the ego. A vile serpent isn't it? It can stop being vicious if you stop feeding it.

The constant need for you to be accurate rather the fearfulness of having to be wrong, the petulant refusal to accept the modernization, the undying need to be conservative,

the astonishing act of censorship and the worst of all, the consistent howling of your refusal to surrender your decisions in front of the younger generation for a mere assumption that we are incompetent, inexperienced, ignorant, is all the meals it craves, it desires and like lost wanderers on a diverged path,

here the load less taken being the curse on our future and the road with the heavier commute being the same, the serpent has become successful in unleashing and spitting its venom out of our future. We, to be factual, are none of it. What I can agree on is that we're not actively competent, experienced, and aware.

However, we can be rather; we will be. Unlike your petty generation, we have the quality and ability to self-realize and progress. While old men with kurtas and a white, dense beard often paired with a bald head, continue to rant and shout like maniacs, we stand still and witness as we fear the word will tumble in front of our mere eyes and when we will try to help,

we will be shut down by your ego, your undying need to be accurate, and how you refuse to accept that even we have the potential to be accurate. We are not just young figures on a clueless journey sir, we are the generation who's ready to fight, unlike yours, which conveniently hides itself behind lushful doors of support as a weak justification for your behaviour. You crumbled our world.

While we watched and suffered, you enjoyed your retirement. I'm not thankful for your generation, I'm livid, but what's done is done, and I will make sure that the reparations are paid, for it is our future, and it is our responsibility to curse and make the culprits realise the immensity of their crimes, and our future cannot even for a brief moment can be gambled with, especially by those who have no relation to it.

Dominance

our voices seamlessly echo within barriers of acceptance. a barrier which has by historical anecdotes defied its purpose and refused to abide by the sole reason it was created. created. hysterical isn't it?

created by mortals to claim themselves above other mortals?

as they blind others with claims of hope and eradicate their stoic nature to preserve their image as bold, present themselves as fierce,

ironically it is their fear which has forced them to reconsider their paths towards progress and establish such barriers which were engineered to help them, yet here they stand, oppressing the common man,

why common you ask, it is because the claimed superior felt the need to throne themselves as the only ones, but the competition evolved, birthing fear and an undying threat of failure.

Delayed Gratification

An undying sense of guilt.
Another unanticipated disaster.
Havoc wreaked on all who desired to contest.
Hindsights highlight disaster, devastation.

A build-up, an instigation. A kindle.
An endless list of hope.
Desire.
For all's too glorious to be a reality.

But our delusion prevents us from it's acknowledgement.
A demolition like no other.

For when his desire will be matched with the apocalypse,
The world will crumble down to the mere fragments from
Which it was born in.

A masterpiece.

A War and a Cup of Chai

Even in the coldest of tundras,
Could you pack enough heat?

So mindlessly colloquial,
Apologies.

For the war occurs in the land of the frozen devil,
Where abandoned defendants weep faint sorrows,

Where our privilege is substituted for their grit.
As blinded policymakers gossip about the weather

Unfashionably late. Perhaps an inevitable devastation rings
But what use? Our cell phones busy

Informing us about the trip to Maldives Bollywood sponsors.
Informing us about the newest divorce in Hollywood.

As the uncles and aunties shame us for marriage, weight.
Pati nahi milega, mota ho gaya hai, gay-way kuch nahi hota

Gibberish, I must say. A political tantrum.
Oh, and what for our misery resides on *their* shoulders!

One casting mistake, and the whole production goes down the drain.
fake promises of us as superstars now turned us into irrelevant extras.

Who produces? Who directs? Who publishes?
Who consumes? Who are we aiming to entertain?
Silence.

Oh, the pistol has struck. A cry for the ambulance.
Hold on kid, we are busy decoding how *Sharma Ji* ka beta scored a perfect score.

Instilling Erudition Within Those Who Understand

Ah, *now* the people witnessed the chaos,
Where is our man of the hour?

Sipping tea?
Well, he's used to it. A historic source of revenue.

Desires to be a podcaster, millennial.
Desires to bring change, millennium.

I wonder how Tarantino would react?
Knowing his legacy is being replicated with real props.

Real figures, real directors. A realistic simulation.
With riots engulfing our tea-time gossip,

Disturbing. Disrespectful.

Oh, *didi* is doing great?

That's amazing! How's the baba in saffron?
Oh, he stopped wearing saffron?

Makes the bloodstains evident, is it?

Understandable. Did dadaji finally grow his beard?

Oh, terrific! I remember how they used to tease me,
Even when I gave them a hug, he was appalled.

I haven't spoken to him in a while,
Is he alright? He better be, we've donated so much blood for him.

Does he still have his househelp, Amitri Bhaiya?
I remember once we were playing cricket, oh what strategies he devised.

I didn't know he could strategise so well,
But he was rather aggressive.

Often he would talk about dividing the field into two aspects.
One side had a large majority, but he never provided anything so resourceful there.

The other side had scarce figures, lethargic in the field.
Perhaps forgotten? Purposely ignored definitely.

Anyways, the audience didn't care about it,
So why should we?

Those were fun times!

How did we have so much monopoly on the points table?

We never lost once we started winning.

Give Atal ji my heartfelt greetings,

Khuda Hafiz.

One's Lure For A Figure.

an endless journey into a definitive pitfall.
pretty foolish, yet the fool must continue, apparently.
for he seeks the gold, the gems, all which have been disguised
from their cursed forms.
oh how pretty he must think they are.
how devastating they stand.
a fool's paradise, his history, his inscription.
our joy.

Armories And Arsenals

why must his journey seem like an endless facade of
mockery?
a fool must entertain, while the intellectuals must educate.
a parade of charades. an act to detach.
parasitic, yet his profession lives on it's cursed virtue.
sir Malcolm, he cries. entertains and goes back into his
shadow of despair. his eyes hide his assault.
his attire unravels the piercingly poignant prophecies,
designed with such astute skill, one cannot replicate.
he has now envisioned his armoury yet again.
a numbed excitement.
his ink shall bleed again, questioning the inevitable.
for Maria, Andrew, or even Toby have failed to given him
thought, dwindling away in their own fantasies.
you've made us laugh, fool.
but your narration is bound to make us weep.

A Glorious Exuberation

another anticipation, another dread.
perhaps this wasn't always the case.
lack of preparation?

once dread turned to hatred, shrewd hatred.
now it stands as lethargy?
even though it shouldn't, one is definitely amused.

it did once spark interest; perhaps it still does.
I fail to recognise. it's a curse- mishap.
a blunder to my glory, for the clock, has struck.

the anticipation must resolve,
for the war now begins.

A Toast To Bradbury's Genius And Our Ignorance

a definite oppression, a definite failure towards one's control over their own.
a constant flurry of desolation.
where that slaughtering autocrat unleashes his onslaught.
chaining everyone to a hook exuberating death.
where the intellectuals are forced to be censored
because money has bought the nincompoops.
where books are burned to ashes, and then those ashes are burned to dust.
anticipating the arrival of a vacuum, which shall grasp all particles with a definitive flurry.
engineering a denouement,
dystopia.

His Roll, His Fate

he too resides in the hopes of delusion.
waiting for his turn,
as the dice determines his fate.
ironically piercing. he's tempted to disrupt the board,
but he must wait. for he is forced to.
an unending wait. it grows.

another fragment joins in, participates.
a vibration, steadily converting into an agitation.
these inscribed puppets, meticulous diagonals.
paint a rather uncanny portrait. a disturbing sign.

give me the gun, he exclaims.
the fools give it too.
dawn, daunt.

A Battle Of No Proportions

he seeks an opportunity to infuse something pure,
for all he possesses is materialism.
and he fears an outbreak. for that seems too explicit.
an imagination, disastrously haunting.
his anger feasts on those devils
deserves recognition.
he will make sure.
prepared, loaded, ready to assault.
exhilaration.

An Unending Agitation

in an unfortunate state of perplexity,
he searches for a resolution,
unfortunately it stands unwavered, undisturbed, indifferent.
a sigh, desperation.
for one gamble rewards wealth, and the other a short-term
boom.
which road is the one less taken?
he knows not, will he ever?
he seeks a denouement,
the map slowly unfolds.

A Hope, A Delusion, A Pain

a pain of knowing the inevitable of not having the one
fragment he desires. a blasphemy, unfortunate.

questioning the attainability of two locked palms,
nurturing their heads as tears gush down their rivers.

the desire for a rivet, a support.
but this is greater. a larger extent.

on an opaque night, where the moon blesses the invisible
figures. gifting light to them who locks palms shares the same
tears, adores, and comforts even after the world crumbles.

A Tumultuous Disruption

this piecing lie, cursed, shrewd.
a constant chaos of determined demolition.
the refusal to witness their defeat.
as the chimes of the shrieks amplify,
my grit is shredded.
my patience is shattered, and one's life
is burnt to dust.

When Love Locked Horns With His Fate

it is indeed a fear, a nervousness.
for he knows that he's experienced a defeat before.
it would indeed be crude to term it s defeat.
reality struck.

he fears another similar onslaught.
an assault to both.
one undeserving, the other pleads guilty.
for his agony is determined to curate his destiny.

funny word,
hopeful, fearful.

A Diminutive Numbness

a sudden numbness,

lack of knowledge.

faint, distant, diminutive.

a shared which pierces.

let it bleed.

endless, overwhelming, ominous.

it seeks the spotlight, as it's ignored gloriously.

Mirror-Mirror On Her Wall

she truly is majestic. amnesty.
deceives us into believing that she is our creation.
as she gently prepares to make us the fools that we are.
transferring us into a load of artificial transport.
as we witness the exquisite of her creations,
travelling the paths she has carefully crafted and carved.
acknowledging the mere true form in which we exist in.
miniature. diminutive. insignificant.

Narrative Sorrows

is it my fault to have been born in a society so relentlessly patriarchal, with an egoistic barrier that prevents them from admitting to be so?

creating a portrait of an "ideal" figure because it appealed to a few, and for the others, it became a mandate?

so egoistic that even the factual remains of science seemed subjective pieces of morality?

astonishing. rather, appalling. one's refusal to admit to being wrong led to a mass following of sorts where everyone assumed him to be factual. him because the ones identifying as "she/her" rather than the ones forced to identify were shamelessly restricted from having access to their own independence?

society, found a cure. they forced them to delude themselves into believing that what in reality was materialism, appealed to them as independence. so they were left helpless. as am i. as are the ones around me who parallel me. not anyone older, nor younger. mere assumptions were catastrophically tossed around as the ignorant sat back and dove into a deceptive pool of amusement?

disgusting. Why do I face the consequences for another man's crime?

however repetitive, it is not justified. I need explanations, but as realism constructs itself before me, i will not get one. because the ones who can provide me one or more and censored by the insecure. afraid that they may speak the truth which will cause their impeachment. they live and prosper while we die and suffer.

His Exhaustion

Encompassed by an ocean of overwhelming waves,
Seeking refuge, refuted by his fate.
Emotions slaughtering that menial diction,
As glorious as one would anticipate,
As demolishing as one would expect.
He deafens himself to the amplified monstrosity which sits beside him,
A mockery of sorts, if the sorts had been so arduously meticulous and infused within him,
Empty canvases, empty paths, all for the eventual ink drought.

A Battle Turned Into A Brawl

The erudite witness a battle of disproportionate proportions,
Acknowledging how wit-fully the hounds must amplify their bark,

Yet aware that their aggression is bound to dominate.
Their barks turn into sinister shrieks,

Crawling up on the bleak yet firm shoulders of those who silently envision.
As the hounds battle their tumult out of their cuffs, strangled.

Tomfoolery is another term.
This, ladies and gentlemen, is a misinterpreted array of acidic assault.

They draft their endings into the dusk of supposedly congenial dusk.
I suppose it still is not too late to use the key.

Democracy

perhaps an endless torment?
seems to be categorised as such perfectly,
yet we fail to assign,
imagine a dystopia with it's inclusion.
our inability, our decision, our failure.
assemble the intellectuals, for their beheading, is soon.

Why Does One Embark On A Journey Premeditated?

a trouble, a realisation.
where the faintest of sirens can deafen.
vulnerable.

viewing a portrait from the valley,
as the clouds dilute his vision,
engulf.

he seeks solutions,
he fears an outcome,
cowardice.

he succumbs,
gives in and surrenders,
fallacy.

Gibberish

an endless chime of hopeless facades
echo and embrace the place of worship.
as our delusion amplifies,
our horrors taunt.

Vulnerability

desolation,

in a state of despair and seclusion.

an appalling silence,

echoes find their own voice.

as my state deteriorates,

seeking refuge,

companionship,

an attempt to avoid the assault.

Farewell

a definite fatigue, weakness.
a lurk within one's introspection.
eerie, filthy.
for the answers aren't within his grasp,
as his wild goose chase takes shape,
the bystander witnesses the parody of our reality.
searching for inner tranquility, he perishes.
as the bystander sweeps all things materialistic
residing as ashes.

Infused Within

A sense of fatigue, weakness.
A desperation for a falsification.
A forgotten anxiousness,
A relapse.

Methods searched for distraction,
Perhaps a seek towards a definitive decision?
An answer? A guiding light towards objectivity?

All's but too frail for this sudden emergence.
No anticipation. Petrifying.
Commonly witnessed across the world,
Now he must endure it too.

A relapse.
A forgotten anxiousness,
A desperation for falsification.
A sense of fatigue, weakness.

Perhaps A Disease

A remedy, perhaps an infatuation.
Relief? Maybe.
Lacks clarity.

Concise, precise, lethal.
For even the greatest of *Ayurvedas*
Cannot explain this parody,

A punishment perhaps,
Perhaps a remedy.
Perhaps.

With No Precaution Comes No Cure

A forgotten ruby, what misery have we birthed here.
An element so poetic, dominated by illusions?

An unpleasant portrait initially,
With a crown one does not desire to be coronated with.

Yet when sawed, oh magnificence!
Mirrors our irrelevance, mere scraps.

An attempt to sculpt it as innumerable statues,
But the representation is immortal.

Our nerves are nothing but two vacant streams,
Veins for certain intellectuals.

We ourselves are a mockery. Mere scraps.
For it shall take nothing but a mere eruption,

A rock, a leakage, or a widespread.
To eradicate each and every mortal soul.

And yet, we have the gall to ignore our perfect mirror.
A mirror highlighting our asymmetry, reality.

Our constructs to beautify us, rather arrogant.
But when our chaos is to be unleashed,

Will we turn to this forgotten ruby,
A source for our nourishment, our mirror,

And regret our sorrows?

Unapologetic

Roses are red,
violets are blue,
one would expect a rhyme to suit their suit,
another example of how blind we stand to others.

perception. curse. murder.

now please do not give me an excuse to "love yourself,"
because the world has made it impossible. impossible.
one tries their best to be sturdy, unfortunately, the quakes of reality cripple him down.
he screams, cries, struggles, all worth for what the worth was below the worth to the worth of none.

his attempts are masked by the world's cruel attempt at success,
ironic and brutal to them be the talk masters of the mastery of selflessness.
demand for their pleasures. pain.

fortunately the world's gift arrived as the elves, enraged, unmuted the curse and so too followed, with the pleasure of painful joy, the script read, he attempted, was abused, and hurled at

he was masked,

strangled,

suffocated,

left aloof, naked,

dead.

and, scene!

Arrogance

It's humourous how our reliance on the superior is built on their reliance over us.

How seamlessly we stand intertwined with an immense love towards ignorance which prevents our vision from acknowledging their contribution.

sure, the rewards have discrepancies; however the level of contribution is believed to be on the same stream.

now one cannot deny it's dominance, and irrespective of the burden, acceptance has to prevail. idealism has astonishingly flourished,

abusing Orwell with every breath it inhales, and it's venom has lashed onto the weak and chokes them till date. why does one rely on such delusions?

pleasure must be seeked however, it is the clutch which shards them effortlessly, continuously, mercilessly.

Inevitable

A repetitive failure,
Doomsday.

A condolence to support.
Pity.

A whine for support,
Desperation.

An irrational argument.
Funeral.

Sunday Afternoon, Overcast.

Tea time with the aunties,

Oh, golly! the intel.

What appeared to be a mindless bicker, an infusion of ecstasy.

Mishra Ji's daughter got a scholarship, Mrs.Patel lost 34 kgs,

Did you see Sharma Ji's son's girlfriend? This youth is spoilt.

Oh, we were the original youths.

India at war with Pa– need I say more?

An unanticipated luxury of unemployed spies exchanging mere words with me.

Oh poor, poor Mr.Amit. How bad was the accident?

An unintroduced whisper, definitely intriguing.

It skips before me.

Rather astonishing. Patience must be key.

My chai loses steam now; patience turns to dread, reality.

The whisper reaches. An error, the spies have failed.

Anticipating To Soar, For She Cannot Be Oppressed

It stands, written on our scriptures, wallowing weakly, whining. Waiting.
Weary of what walls widowed from the passage of Progress possess.

Tumultuous trembles, tormented throughout, troubled, torn.
Trying to transition into terrifying terror. Dancing dauntingly, deemed down to destruction.

For who stands responsible?
The Superior?
Oh, how amusing that would be.

As we constantly erode *Her* beauty,
Eradicate *her* soul,
Excavate extracts engulfing *her* dignity, extortion.

She stands suffocated. Sufficed by sufficient sinners.
From devastating dictators to ruthlessly ravishing rebels,
She has endured it all.

All our curses, boiled and plated on *her* neck,
As we slither with venom residing on our tongues,

Waiting to assault *her*.

Our curses, our thoughts, our destruction, *her* responsibility.
Our devastation, *her* instigation.
Our wars, *her* casualty.

For when Destiny knocks,
He will be the Antigone to his sister's burial.

Her wings, now spread, seeking a soar with Phoenix.
Defeatist of another opportunity,
For she is glorious,
She is,

Society.

Will There Be Soft Rains?

are we enveloped by the inevitable curse of Teasdale?
will we *perish utterly*?
for it does seem apt. our ignorance, mistaken for bliss.
while nature eyes the innocent fool,
preparing for the ambush,
deemed to leave us defenseless.

Memories

A burning nostalgia rests on that bleak cubed flesh.
The flame evokes that certain grin,
As expected, yet still, *that* grin promotes pleasure.
Appalling to the bystander who watches me enjoy,
As he cries for help, disturbing.
The flame persists; perhaps it wants me to enjoy?
The grin never dies,
Nor does the nostalgia.

An Alphabetical Anagram

Agony assaults the astonished Anger.
Brawling brutally before the burdensome battle.
Constantly cawing for cowardice calls.
Deemed to doom, daunts the dawn.

Emphatically energetic, anticipating eagerly.
Ferociously furious, for she fears the foresight.
Gnawing. Gruesome gallons of ghostly grants loom.
Hinting hatefully, hunched by hope.

Instilled within indifferent insights,
Jubilance jolts hurriedly jostled.
Knowing keenly how knavish kings are.
Lurking within the lumps of lure,

Masking the muttered murmur masterfully.
Not knowledged about neither norms
Oppressed obnoxiously by olfactory obstacles.
Perceiving precariously, prejudiced perhaps.

Quantitative quality, she has quilted her dance.
Rumbling ruthlessly, ravishing righteously.
Sinfully slithering slyly, for she walks silently.
Ultimately ulterior or uniquely ubiquitous?

Venomously verifying our viscosity.
Wailing, whining, wholesomeness wiped.
Xylophones exemplified exert their exemption.
Zooming zeals, now distant, zonally farewelled.

Neo Politics

a heavy strum, an alarm, a suggestion.

upbeat, provocative, intimidating.

a deafening silence to the numb echo.

a sudden burst, incompetence highlighted.

the lap continues, for the distance is yet to be completed,

call them leaders,

astonishment. suffering. delusion. inevitability. reality.

Confusion

you don't have to be beautiful in order to succeed.
similarly you don't have to succeed in order to be beautiful.
it's about how you perceive yourself, and if you perceive
yourself as beautiful,
you're gonna be beautiful forever.

your torment is devastating,
to witness, to understand, to recover.
You must, must acknowledge your prowess, kid,
The world does not wait every day to be conquered.

Attempt Number 7

oh for what may be,
near the edge of the cliff.

terrified. as courage seeks to soar.
hailing his majesty to the lost wanderers,
exemplifying his wings as he envisions his path.

rambling. indecisive. hesitant.
oh for what may be.
originally, he wasn't meant to.
frightened, realising he must.
terrified.
onyxes seem pale yet opaque.
pursuing his last feel of the luke-warm breath,

soaring endlessly.

Simplicity Redefined

A deafening noise, chaos, disruption, torment.

Guilt rides on the hands of those who sculpt masterpieces.
Unexampled, inimitable hence the jealousy.
Irking those incompetent traditionalists, who fail to acknowledge it's genius.
Devastated by the grace it births. Perplexing him, he who inaugurated brilliance.
Exquisite. They call him Mike, I still prefer Michael.

Three areas engulfed with beauty, a realisation of our abusive luxuries.
Omnipresent, yet we turned the blind eye towards the denouement.

Meticulously juvenile. A luxury seems mystical.
Indeed it can be after it finishes exerting its venom.
Needlessly wasteful for us to chase the chaos.
Incidentally tormenting? Abusive? Greed.
Mindless. Where the chaos personifies, we mustn't be fragile.
Adequacy has never gifted anyone grace, yet his strokes did.
Lamination towards the answer to our burdens. Three souls of elegance.
Iconography to the bare, even Eloquence fails to understand.

Symmetrical perfection, five strokes, finesse.

Minimalism.

Unheard Hopes

I miss those rocky tiles glistening against my patched heel.

Healing my reminiscence of natural beauty, organic beauty.
Olfactory senses of my grandma's Jollof rice and egusi soup take shape.
Persisting against my ever-tempted quench,
Exemplifying culture, glamour, and enchant.

The torso of my body is now proud.
Openly announcing it's flatulence.

Reminding me of those excavated topazes
Existing in my realm. Hopeful delusions.
Turning the tables, oh the plywood on which I ate.
Unwavered by the political mess, my grandma, the food, the culture.
Rendering my hopes to the shattering reality.
Nevertheless, I must enjoy the biscuits and tea now.

Goodbye, darling.

Dear Diary

Oh, those gruesome figurines of wax
now seem to leave no scar.

Demolition has mocked it's the last laugh
as perseverance led me to these horrors.

oh how I miss England!
but those blokes there would never understand.

ah, guess this was just another day in the basket,
it's time to return to the office now.

oh these visuals would greet me,
oh i know.

what has one traded for this merciless life of displeasing
pleasures?
Will one ever know?
anyways, one must endure the blood of capitalism
and mimic their wishful thinking of Marxism.

I hope to live long enough to meet you again.
toodles!

Complexity Intertwines With Mystery

Relative to the layman, often appeased by the erudite.
Extravagant to those who preach it's very existence.
Like honestly, the Egyptians have perplexed the very minds
Associated with the foundations of the assumed universe.
Tick-Tock– the sound of their nightmares. Fundamentally fallaciousness
Instigate their agitation further. Appallingly amusing.
Vicious, exclaims the layman. Beautiful, claims the edifice.
Extravagant? It scorches the minds, as one fails to understand.

On the other hand, well, one cannot claim. As
Relative as it may be, it is ironically universal.

Now entities differ. She herself was one.
Overwhelming. Agitating.
Trouble taunts her, for the layman still fails to understand.

Questions pile on.
For,

Is tomorrow really a mystery?
And can the past really be history?

Governance

A revenge? An annihilation.

A striking thunder on my vulnerable hut, diminutive.
An agitating roar, a rumble, enormous.
Failing to attract, dominate. Casting a definite fear.

A tsunami of fear, definitely not the only captive.
But the only one to acknowledge the suffering,
And call for a revolution.

Defending Solo

Oh what pity you unleash on me now!
You stand unaware of the consequences, the assault which berates upon me consistently!
Your negligence, incompetence, drives the killers free, drives them with absolute abomination.

I was the queen. But seemingly the venomous land of Bandhavgarh descended to disrespect me,
It was, it is, it will always be my throne! You're no one to decipher my success.

A great act of violence, an encroachment, so vivid, so horrifying.
Claw marks on my coronation, a duration– encompassed with horrors and—sigh.

Those instilled pecan pearls alongside a signature tattoo, a mark of originality,
Now bleed of an annihilation you couldn't have imagined.

A muted narration of my story, for the causes are unknown?

A battle was fought, gloriously. Bamera Junior, a vile curse. A pawn versus the queen.

How'd he expect to defeat and defy? Sure certain strands of blood painted his abuse,
His father, a maniac. Eyeing on *my* poor, precious cubs to assert his domination. Coward.

The world introduced censorship. You all, ignored. The spread of a menial parasite, you.
My territory, eyed for gold. Ignored about how poetic and glamorous I perceive it to be. Oh, the pain!

For your ignorance only compliments my loss, realisation?

Having to succumb to the threats of the very dominating males.
Having to depart from *my* throne!
Oh, for my weeps aren't sufficient.

For the throne was bound to be abused.
And I was bound to lose.

And now that I *finally* have, *you* know not why.

A Basic Search For Adrenaline

You say you've walked through one fire.
Seems daring enough.

Now question, halt and reflect.
Are you willing to walk through another one?
Can you find a way out?
Are you willing to be the victim to the scorching torment yet again?

Marjan Miyaan

Who'd have expected you to be this cruel?
Entertaining an endless facade of suffering.
Ad your politically driven nonsense chimes, and deafens our mercilessly degraded soul
Turning us i to a suffering of your sufferings is fallacious,
For our roars, our stance, and our vision, is enough to apply a diaper on your display of cowardice.
A land filled with suffering, and we are the victims.
Ironic, when read your zoo's name in a dialect, a dialect so pure,
Yet, we disobey the translation. Our death lies in your bureaucracy.

And we shall roar again, a feast shared with our brothers.

A Frail Battleground

A failed search towards another definite answer,
A longed freedom, aggression.
Understood? A brawl, a fight, endless dedication.
One must, if needed, exceed one's expectations to prove a point.
A barrier to one's thoughts, the one motive.
The one opportunity,
The one battle.

A Halted Flight

pure melodies gain a song bound to awaken, shun.
a realisation sparks within,
as gunshots, tightropes and destruction seem mere sources of adrenaline.
an attempted distraction, delays the realisation.
ineffective. really, a display of anger is misunderstood as a long for freedom is sought after with utmost desperation.
but he knows, unfortunately, he's merely a bird, confined within the cages of reality. the harder he attempts to escape, the more damage he inflicts upon his wings.

Written Near A Port, On A Bright Afternoon

Could you be someone's breath when they sink in the deepest of waters?
Could you be their torch when the cave shuns all light?
Could you be their support when they hang from the steepest cliff?
Mere irrational arguments.

Enough to claim love? Chaotic isn't it?

Can you claim your love over theirs?

Written near a port, on a bright afternoon,
Enough to spark a realisation within.

Proud And Alive

A mesmerising depiction of one's beauty, a follow-up of *charades.*
Vile, vicious, venomous, frivolous. Those rumours, facades.

It's his escapade, isn't it? Your inaudible murmur, cowardice.
What one wouldn't have expected has showered us.

A depiction of our ignorance, relentlessness.
His constant attempts at his defence, left him breathless.

As his corpse takes life,
With pride, his flag resides. An inaudible echo, a fife.

Not your possession, neither one to be commented upon,
For we're mere scraps on one's plate,
And he who supposedly resides upon us?
He doesn't. For education and morality,
Have diminished us into mere pawns.

A curse to love, a curse to celebrate.
We aren't fragmented figures for you to castigate.

A Definitive Solution

A vile seclusion. A rather endless list. What might one be able to encapsulate,
Or translate such a venomous display. An anticipation erupts, as time taunts.

It dances on its own paper-thin strings, which long to be broken. Now, who controls?
Who must be poisoned in order to instigate freedom for this sorrowful soul?

Another anticipation builds, this time with glee and viciousness. A smirk, a burnt Cuban cigar.
A pungent pain, a pleasure? Perhaps. Pecan portraits, lying idle, perpetually penetrating.

The smirk widens, envisions the cocktail topped with poison.
A lone leaf, emerald.
Complimenting the glam of the iced thirst-quencher, pleasing.

One sip, the second.
Thirst quenched.

The Sky Too, Eats The Land At Home

A downpour, an obliteration. Unleashing a definite catastrophe on those who dare to fool themselves in it's admiration. A pluviophile lives in denial. For it is indeed acidic. No, he exclaims.

A deafening murmur is no sign of enchant, but an assault. Fitting name yet again.

Blanketing the fields with a curse, a hope, a delusion, a pain.
A realisation had before.

For the desperate anticipate, and adore it's glory,
As it envelops the slums, the poor, and the vulnerable,

And eats the land at home.

A Sudden Overwhelming

A scenario never imagined before,
a burden failing to be pacified.
It crumbles his miniature figure,
as he braces himself to an inevitable distraction.
Shall he succeed?
Overwhelmed by even the thought of grasping the scenario.

The Anticipated Departure?

lying on the bed, glued by those vile thorns.
built on the frozen ink of the dullards who were so enthusiastic to give the world another worthless sacrifice.

their impatience drove them towards a forgotten land.
It feasts on their incompetence, their vulnerability.
As glittered offers of peace and tranquility flurry, all for their graves.

Is that the walk of life?

As one enters this cauldron of chaos,
They're displaced into a state of sterility.
For the battles are unchained too,
And one lacks the arsenal.

An assault with encumbering tallies,
Now engulf the poor layman,
As he attempts to infuse Zeus,
Fails, sinks, halts.

Fate Neither Dictates, Nor Influences

Confined within a prison of torment, lacking elegance so vividly.
Surrounded by the recurring constructs,
preventing the growth of another robotic creation.
a stunted progress, lacking elegance so vividly.

A sense of suffocation, now grasps his once longed determination.
An initial boom, a success, an escape from the means of this confinement.
Now an enveloping bust, a trough of his degeneracy. Another menial construct,
Another hapless creation, insignificant to those who reside around him.

A pungent smell, fairly toxicating. The source stands unknown. One's failure
At his success or his success at their failure? A dilemma one cannot solve.
For one's success is vital, so is their failure - or so as they say. A path leading
To destruction and desolation, yet he chooses to pursue - a pursuit of gloom.

The sky turns grey, gray. Lost in translation he fails, fails to embrace his shrill, diminutive, frail
voice, masked successfully by the roar of the bolting sight, an irregular one indeed. Spotlights a certain ambush, a showcase so vivid and blinding, it pains. The source, still unknown. One eye witnesses the lush, the lush of the lustrous fields, the other sees emigration. Whom to trust?

A few miles ahead lies a dry land, oxymoronic of the gift he was presented with earlier.
Innumerable cracks, soft, hungry? Soaking in every tourist, allowing them to experience its curse,
His eyes are forced to witness only one picturesque view now. No scene to compare with, insufficient diction to comment, he must simply acknowledge. A scorching guiding light, thirst.

Finds himself in the divide. One side reflects the wealth, enchant, greed and filth, attracts and nurtures? Guarantees glee, for even he, is not so gullible, but he is definitely human. The other projects complete blandness - neither glee nor gloom. A perfect middle-ground.
He must choose (perhaps, but is it his gullibility making it seem so?), for he has nowhere else to turn to.

Falling In Love With None

Isn't it a simple cliché?
Stealing stars, ah– how can I even progress without a sense of disgust?

Romanticizing the idea of love? Extraordinary.
An ache residing without any aid.

A sense of frivolity, gut-wrenching fear, appal.
All now categorised under the phenomenon of love.

A choir of oppression, of tumult, of a failed diction.
Seeks aid, it lies beside, yet clichés and repetitive parlance dominates.

Ah (chuckles).

The Sequel

A yearn for a delicious redemption,
Inappropriate adjective, but the quality must be relished.
For he has fought a battle one wouldn't have expected,
Contesting familial blood, losing or winning, one is unknown.
Definitely prevented from succumbing.

Instigated by a cruel prospective father-figure, who laughs maniacally
On the diabolic failure of his kingdom. Cursing freely on Zeus' greatness, tomfoolery.

I strive to make those dullards taste what they have left to rot.
For when it rots, the sourness is personified. A rather perfect redemption.

Contesting him again, for the kingdom. It was his greed; now it shall be
Met with my thirst, anger. My eyes have never seen such a glow, and perhaps
Never will again. I must incorporate all the gall the thick knight has bestowed upon me,
And march towards glory. For Glory herself anticipates my arrival, and I do not strive to disappoint.

You shall witness my ravishing assault–

on the battlefield when I contest, and after, when I celebrate.

Army!

Prepare for battle.

Reload And Shoot

A faint portrait, a faded mesmerisation.
Failed to be intercepted by all the intellectuals.
For they are monotonous features, accomplishing nothing but menial calculations.

For their delusion leads them to forgo their humanity, emotions, a connection even.
A moment to acknowledge, a lifetime to admire.
A faint portrait, a faded mesmerisation.

A faint portrait, a faded mesmerisation.
A gift by nature, and we stand so inappreciative.
Don't we know that where she gifts, she wreaks havoc too?
Only takes a command.

How can one have ever achieved such a height of perfection?
A newer brand of genius.
Endorsing their constructs as well. recalcitrance.
A faint portrait, a faded mesmerisation.

A faint portrait, a faded mesmerisation.
Faint strokes, diluted canvases.
A demolition of beauty.
Reluctance.

Ignorance,

Hesitance,

Aversion,

Ignorance.

Unforgivable,

A repetitive curse,

A faint portrait,

a faded mesmerisation.

A Request For You To Understand

Another tea-time session, I suppose? Drinking coffee today, are we?
How has *Sharma-Ji* been? Moving on.
You don't require any hearing aid or power glasses, do you?
Just wanted to clear an important doubt.

So, I had one small issue. A minor inconvenience, if I may.

How does it matter to the world what my breakfast, lunch or dinner has been?
Ultimately the goal is for me to satisfy my hunger, right?
Apologies for my crudeness, but I had to resort to your level of pettiness,
For unless a mirror is bashed on your head, you do not seem to understand.

Coming back to the concern at hand.
I genuinely do not think that the packet of crisps that I eat would increase your fat intake.
I would definitely be appalled, and more than anything, disdained if that occurred.
But since it does not, why does my dietary input affect your health?

Menial comments, Meenal aunty, seriously? I mean, aren't you the one who runs a salad bar?
Well, and how does my wobbly appearance affect your look in the mirror?
It is not like when you take a mirror-selfie, as you blanket yourself with mined gems,
I appear and taint the quality of the image. The flash is enough to hide a majority of your bragging.

It definitely does evoke curiosity, and yes, I constantly wonder now, out of concern,
If we could erase unemployment for the elderly and especially you all, for you guys
Immediately need to eradicate wasting your priceless time on critiquing filthy imperfectly
Constructed figures such as myself, and go out there and change the world.

For, only those who are forcefully spotlighted as the perfect figure succeed?
I wonder who rules us? I wonder who once called us from the other side?
Your beauty was not seen then.

Or had you forgotten,
Your perfectly built *beta* had failed too.

We pursued different ways, dear aunties, uncles, parents, friends, and families,
It doesn’t matter if you take the one less taken,
For any assault is bound to erode even the purest of gold.

Temptations

A day without any burdensome battles,
A rather silent boredom.

A domination, a havoc waiting to be wreaked.
But no sign to be seen here.

He's lost in the wait of the hope,
But this lost and won battle, seems long-gone.

The awakening of the shields,
The anarchy of these carved, blood-fed swords.

All these bodies displaced on the ground without hope,
War-fought cowards, self-centred, betrayers.

For they knew that another battle was to be fought,
But they unleashed their plethora of prowess in this one.

Couldn't they have waited as well?
What will our children learn? To finish one battle before another?

Chaotic. Disruptive, a failure to engage. For what *is,*
'Too good, to be'– a bloody tomfoolery!

A rather scorching agitation, a ravishing anger.
Your bloody scoundrel-like workers shall be a victim too.

Oh for don't you ever have the gall to curse yourself with my innocence,
For you shall witness too, how your blunders are my weaponry.

And when the assault shall be rained upon you,
You shall burn to the ground with your ashes, suffocated.
You have made the debacle of letting me long,

For another bloody scoundrel, sharpens his sword.

Not Just Another Water Body

Why are you only awake when my sea turns into an attraction?
For a bleed must be exercised for your attention.

Those monstrous storms, disruptive tsunamis, avalanches,
All forsaken. For I am your witness only when your discretion admits.

An annihilation had just elapsed, but I don't assume you cared to acknowledge?
A curse, truly. Better run then, these reefs do not sense anger out of a bolt.

Would you look at what you've done? My poor, poor sea-turtles are now infused
With your pollution. The only curiosity, the chief pollutant seems missing.

Oh so you want to admire my beauty *now*?
What happened when your precious factories went on a stroll?
Or should I remind you of your dear friend, Plastic?
Congratulations, as the food you desire, is now instilled with your filth.

Just because you had me displaced in a fancy, distant location in Australia,
Does not mean that my anger would be pacified.

Oh, you poor soul, my devastation would see life.
Pray, and by all means *pray*, that the waves do not reach the shore.

Because, that is all you can do.

A Stream of Desolation

What curse might this exhaustion entail?
A definite loss. Might be exhaustion, might be a
misunderstanding.
A hope to turn it into a misunderstanding.
Mere diction, unfailing repetitions,

For you cannot learn to appreciate water till the well is dry,
But why must we soak the essence it has gained life on?
A powerless parade.

A stampede of illusions,
Delusions, a stream of desolation.

The Colosseum

This battle is being longed to be fought,
For the daring soul encounters the composed fool.

An eye for deception, a wish towards a distraction.
Now, what might one say, witness, or endure?

The colosseum shall erupt, with flags soaring seamlessly,
A brutal brawl between two unlikely contestants.

A failure to anticipate unless one is vulnerable.
Will the deck of cards show a shredded pair?

Or will one trump over the other's triumph?

A Torn Note

'Tis the land of the free? Still anticipates an augmented argument.
Hosting a series of mere caricatures, now how must one sit still.

The laughter explodes; please realise that. One must've thought that
The successors would attain rationality at one point, but the tomfoolery still exists.

Where a lump of uneducated deludes set out to decide the fate of a nation,
And cast their assurance on an electoral catastrophe.

A desperation to waterboard number thirty-seven, an odd feeling– why have I developed
A hatred towards numbers? Number forty-five, forty-six, all spark a sense of disgust,

And those are just to name a few. Mathematics has cursed, but the bigger curse still
Resides on the other side of the world. For number forty-seven has brought doom into reality.

The world crumbled at its feet, the *whole* world?
A saffron success on two sides now,

Half of the world has now been encapsulated within it's venomous fist,
With the unfailing, repetitive echo, calling us, it's 'friends,'

What a parody.
As his name echoes, Mo–

A Daily Affirmation To Cure Your Sorrows

If you ever wish to displace your sorrowful sand,
Which lies in your fist, as your grasp tightens–
And you continue to tighten your assurance on your glee.

But oh, you innocent child!
Your sorrows enlighten your surroundings with despair.
But if you wish to ensure that that very lump of sand vanishes,

Loosen your grasp and gain control.
If you wish to unravel the gems within,
Feel free to infuse them within me.

A daily affirmation, although cursed, is ensured.
To be the bearer of your sorrows, to be the reason for your smile,
To be the builder of your success, to be the audience to your conquering.

Censored Intellectuals

A shriek, a howl of desperation.
A longing for a translation.
A misunderstanding masquerading as sympathy.

If you wish to inform, do so with utmost diligence.
A *deathless death* he demands,
Why must he choose this path of irrationality?

Are we standing blind to a catastrophe?
An annihilation instigated by our ignorance,
Bound to plague and ravage?

That can't be right. Hence, we shall blame these foolish Minorities.
After all they are the ones cursing us, aren't they?

We are completely innocent. *We* have never abused.
Oh, how foolish, how infuriating.

A grown beard, the same stench.

How Would You React?

To whomsoever, this may concern,
I am as apologetic for the following convoluted confrontation,
As you are for your banishing beliefs.

How would you react, knowing your only prodigal successor,
Does not want to, have to, or need to comply with social norms?
That they are willingly accepting the methods of progress?
If a search for a groom is gifted with a bride? Or the other way round?

How would you react, knowing your only prodigal successor,
Does not want to, have to, or need to comply with social norms?
That they are forgoing any attachment to the faith, you hold?
If they choose to accept the methods of rationality?

How would you react, knowing your only prodigal successor,
Does not want to, have to, or need to comply with social norms?
That they hindered their preconception into a channel of acceptance?
If they chose to represent themselves with the fabric of those who are not?

How would you react, knowing your only prodigal successor,
Does not want to, have to, or need to comply with social norms?
That they are daring enough to forgo your reliance?
If they chose to pursue the path of independence, irrationality?

Would you still choose to accept?
What if these traits sparked within the neighbour's successor?
How would you react?

I know you have chosen a reaction, for I have been witness to a confession.
Now, when would you be informing the world of your regression?

Another Hopeless Romantic, Another Heartbreak

I do desire the covetous longing to have the fallen strands of the golden thread grace my
ever-so-abandoned desert filled with frail cactuses. a scorch has blessed us yet.

Now we wait for the golden dew to nourish. but I do hold hopes for that one envy,
which the Germans have described as an opportunity to view as attainable.

I try to instigate it at every soul-filled heartbreak I endure, some are so convoluted, I fail
to recognise them. indeed a torment. maybe a wait was the prescription longed for?

a personified prescription is the Middlemist to abundance. yet can I, rather should I strive
for it? Indecision, a thief of opportunity. funny how fate blends the silently muted.

what do I await?
a curse of romance,
an exhilaration of reality.

Lost Soul

It is my dire request to you heartfelt lost wanderers of the faint light,
Choose to not treasure any gem,

For when the neighbours are informed and worry not because they *will* be,
They shall unleash all their prowess on your disjointed soul.

They will strive to snatch, to distribute, and depart as your gem now stands helpless.
The ruby stands host to a portrait of fainted lines, a faint memory.

A gushing down of sorority, a realisation of despair, a futility of replacement.

The inevitability of loss.

Communication

Have you ever wondered where all the forgone souls go?
For after they are forgone, they are not to be audited.

However, the agony arises, when we grieve over our own ignorance.
For we have seen them depart before our own eyes.

We carved their pathway towards the advanced inevitable.
They chose to pursue this journey when we were busy being the audience.

We choose to cry in despair, experiencing all as the thunder strikes
Timelessly. But wouldn't it have helped if you had spared an ear?

Our eyes are nothing but mere spectators. They are mute to these assaults
And moot to the aid. They cannot speak, hear or inform.

We have trusted these fools long enough to know the disdain it wreaks upon us.
And the community lies on the brink of devastation.

Shouldn't we now excavate the tumult?
Scrap out all which infuses itself as shards,

Spare an ear, and listen?

A Scarce Rarity

The one, yes, the only secluded, prominent one– a strand of support.
A pageant for empathy, sympathy, fancier diction. Now unexercised.
Hysterical to them, for they have eradicated the birch on which I relaxed.
Perhaps it is this lethargy that has led me to believe that this birch shall remain forever.

A fatigue which proudly parades on my pale, frail forehead.
For a sight, my eyes are told to behold. A piece of astonishment.
They truly are admirable. Golden birches– as scarce as one would imagine.

But with rarity comes desire; greed. A desire to overpower, perhaps.
Seems attainable as an army is no match for this futile bas–

Never shall I choose to exclaim. To attain a sense of calm, and progress.

Misrepresented Excellence

A picture, a really disturbing one indeed.
Crafted by the miraculous idolaters,

Preaching a masterpiece of perfection,
As blurred realities intertwine themselves

Within the threads of an overwhelming gush of hatred.
For it is to be sold later, wondering how it can be measured?

A group of illiterates will bid their fortunes on beauty,
Unaware of whether perfection can be monetised.

For is it truly perfection, if the eventual goal is to sell?
A longing for change? For change, too, dwindles itself on the lost path.

A constant error, as we speak, it persists,
Determined to grasp one's once imagined glory.

And crumble it to shards, a puzzle bound to fail
Before the naked human eye.

Compared Similarities

A resistance to understand, a lack of translation.
Beware, for this is no misinterpretation, definitely a definite precaution.
For the vision is shadowed by different terminologies,
An unending chaos. A constant pinpoint at their misfortune.

How must they now endure this venomous viscosity?
A chuckle, aiming to tempt a futile eruption.
A day passed by, another exhaustion lived.
Now they endure the critique of the soldiering farmer,

Who has endured the searing calefaction and now aims to
Justify through the suffering of the one who yields.
Two very different journeys lived, but neither are to be understood.
A volcanic disappointment, a blister to doom.

Scars//Doom

the first attempt at a dare,
one of the only excavates marking history.

a day long gone, yet only half experienced.
a death, a relapse, a progress, and a fall,

all mere tools of his daily narrations.
one would expect to him having grown accustomed,

but those who truly underscore his doom know,
a narration so filthy with an underappreciated title

seems close to a wasted ink flow.
he's grown tired, but exhaustion is a first.

The Pillar of Our Dreams

A melodic bashing of those who have strived only to instill education within us.
It goes without the requirement of objectivity to understand their limits.

A refined construction, masterfully crafted in order to help progress,
Now stands, stands– on the verge of a crumble, with nothing but indignity.

A howled exaggeration,
Represented as a pillar of our dreams.

Oh, how they deluded us into its attraction,
But is it their limit that crumbles it further?

A howled exaggeration,
Represented as a pillar of our dreams.

Oh, how they promised land of dignity,
A platform where intellectuals interacted.

A howled exaggeration,
Represented as a pillar of our dreams.

Oh, how they wished we had established ourselves,
For all are lost in a narration of their own pride.

A howled exaggeration,
Represented as a pillar of our dreams.

Curiosity

If anyone ever asks you,
Tell them what a mess we made of art.

If anyone ever asks you,
Tell them what a disaster we made of education.

If anyone ever asks you,
Tell them the chaos we instilled within serenity.

If anyone ever asks you,
Emphasize the tumult we created with politics.

If anyone ever asks you,
Elaborate on our demolition of sophistication.

If anyone ever asks you,
Inform them about the impatience we hold.

If anyone ever asks you,
Instill a sense of wisdom within them.

If anyone ever asks you,
Shun their curiosity, force a curation of solutions.

Narration

I met a group of bold intellectuals the other day,
Found them unorthodox, for they instructed the way
I must progress. For how must I leave my work astray.
Indeed, I was perplexed too. A comment with an array
Of indignification. A lack of comprehension– worn proudly as
if it were a beret.

I have indeed inhaled the smoke of reality: 'Need not be
as esprit, just enough to display patience'. A momentary be–,
Beguiling. For to endure criticism is understood, but a bawbee
Of such nature was unintroduced. Leaving me to question,
even be–,
Believe the torment there is to be.

They're called *Government,* actually. An ordinary name, no
sycee.
Yearly, an electoral process is followed. They take pride,
oversee
Any other aspects which dare to interfere. I dare not to resee,
For they do hold immense intellect (don't they), who is the
devisee
Of their reign? For they are old, fragile, vulnerable. Who is
our new promisee?

You do not seem particularly engaged? Perhaps a sense of hatred? A grandee?
They are no noblemen, at least not yet. You must understand. They're your vendee.
Couldn't you have also pursued the path of greatness? Become an effendi?
Did the plot dilute mid-way? For all is nothing but your engagement, your solidi.
I agree, to banish and bash is no solution, but when the Forzandi
dominates, one must adopt other pathways, employ the glissandi!

A Simple Narration Of A Damsel In Distress

A sudden flurry of numbness,
In Loch Ness, a damsel in distress.
She wails, cries, howls, growls,
A simple narration of a damsel in distress.

For is it Loch Ness?
We must be mistaken, lack the necessary prowess,
Wooed by these filthy dunces,
Who was appreciated for her beauty once,
Is now the king's damsel in distress.

For it is merely a crowd,
Even though hold only pennies, not well endowed,
But seem like spears, bullets, torches,
Determined, as they unleash their disturbing forces.

A sudden flurry of numbness,
In Loch Ness, a damsel in distress.
She wails, cries, howls, growls,
A simple narration of a damsel in distress.

She sees the gentleman *she* desires,
As he fails to acknowledge her glance, a momentary pain,

For does that maniac know not about who requires
Him? She still holds her beauty, unfortunate to have been in
Loch Ness.

A sudden flurry of numbness,
In Loch Ness, a damsel in distress.
She wails, cries, howls, growls,
A simple narration of a damsel in distress.

Crackers

While we're at it, as the youth may say,
Festivals are auspicious, but only in a certain way.

To me, they are plain appalling, as radical as it may be,
Idealistic viewpoints and political convenience,
Demolition of realism, truly.

Now they do provide a sense of comfort, but it's fictional,
really.
Relying on a fictional force to guide us through, really?

Till now, this may have seemed like another festive rant,
But only to those fooled by the curse of Kant.

The Midnight Crescent

a midnight crescent rests on the bleakness
of the chaotic numbness. a glittering silver,
a fool's purchase. a paradise of delusion.
there lies the island of the helpless,
it observes faintly behind the shadows of the blinding light,
a foamed opaqueness. it approaches the traveller,
lurking a lure as it presents itself in magnificence and
grandeur,
the resemblance to a snarl which desires,
awaits a growl - howling on pain of the suffering.

Afterword

It is my immense pleasure to have entertained you through this publication. I fail to verbalise my overwhelming, as my gratitude speaks before me.

This book, in particular, represented certain personally endured events, and it is indeed my fulfillment to have presented it to the world.

Hoping to have allowed you to enjoy through this collection as the warrior within you prepares for the battle.

For I know, each and everyone who has scalped through this collection is unfailingly worthy of possessing the throne of their triumph.

It does seem like a burden to endure the pain with every step, with every breath– however, and as piercing as this may seem to listen, you shall strive to continue. The opponent only feasts at your mercy, and the hungrier you keep it, the weaker it shall get.

It is nothing but a coward who uses you as a shadow, a protection to not alarm the intellectual within. For even it knows, when the intellectual is awoken, they will cast the most scintillating light on the shadow and dissolve it to ashes.

As difficult as the opponent may seem, you should know that your armory holds the arsenal to combat the greatest forces to have ever existed.

Flaunt your arsenal,
For the armoury indeed holds the rarest solitaires.